Your Headline Sucks!

How To Write The Perfect Headline Using This Proven Step by Step Formula

Nick Drzayich & Jake Thompson

DEDICATION

We've learned a lot from a ton of bright and intellectual people
– you know who you are. Thank you all so much!

Contact information:
Nick Drzayich & Jake Thompson
TheClickAuthority.com
800-321-1636

CONTENTS

ACKNOWLEDGMENTS

To those whose work has taught us so much and continues to educate – we hope to influence as many as you.

CHAPTER 1

THE POWER OF GOOD COPYWRITING

If the goal of your business is to sell something, which I'm assuming it is, then copywriting is an integral part of getting whatever it is you want sold, sold.

Now I don't care if you're knocking door-to-door, selling over the phone, selling on the Internet or licking stamps and sending letters to the masses, you need good copywriting.

The power of good copywriting can take any mediocre business, in any industry, and turn them into a giant. I'm not kidding! Some of the best copywriters in the world have taken "decent" businesses and turned them into industry leading behemoths.

In fact, some of the greatest business people I know have small, or more accurately, tiny businesses. They are fantastic at what they do, but horrible at translating that value through marketing and good copy. They stay small because they aren't good copywriters and marketers.

It's what bridges the gap between you and your customer, and it's vital to building a successful business.

Here's something interesting. I'm an avid iPhone user, like many of you, and I would never think of use anything else...or so I thought.

Just the other day Amazon caught my attention with a headline that introduced their new "Fire Phone" and the allure of a full year of Amazon Prime. That lead me to a sales page that introduced, for the first time ever, Amazon's newest smartphone.

I kid you not, by the end of that sales page I wanted one! I wanted to dropkick my iPhone off a cliff just to have an excuse to get on board with the new Amazon Fire Phone.

Now let me point out something important. Amazon had a great product, like many of you do. Great copywriting is not a solution for poor products or poor services.

The point of copywriting is to do one thing:

Make me keep reading so I *see* the great product for what it is.

Great copywriting and great marketing will do nothing for a poor product!

On the flipside, good copywriting can turn an unknown product into a must-have, hot selling, coveted product. It has the power to increase value, decrease competition, and push yourself into a greater share of your market. In other words, good copywriting has the ability to persuade your customers to give you more money for what you sell, and see more value in it.

Now copywriting is a can of worms. There is so much you can learn, and so much you *should* learn...

…but that's not what this book is about.

This book is about a very specific area within copywriting, that is arguably the most important element of copywriting altogether. It's an area that, if you don't do it well, your prospects will arguably never read another word on your page.

It's the headline.

So if you want to learn how to craft killer headlines that will give your readers no other choice but to keep reading, then you've got the right book.

Still reading? Okay great, here we go!

In the following pages and chapters I'm going to lay out for you the key elements and essential pieces to crafting the perfect headline.

Now you might be wondering why I would spend an entire book on such a small portion of sales copy. Well, like I said, the headline is the most important part of any sales copy. The headline is the first thing your potential customer sees. Plus, this is hardly a novel – its meant to be read and implemented in an afternoon.

It's also where people make the biggest mistakes and lose potential customers.

Understanding how to craft a killer headlines will also embody the rest of your message, and help keep you and your audience focused on what they need/want, and what you offer.

The problem, however, is most people do it wrong. They use headlines as summaries for their content, a pitch for their product, or worse, a way to simply rank with keywords for search engines.

This is *not* how you craft a winning headline.

And in a second, I'll go deeper into the real job of a headline, but before I do, I want to mention something important so you can get maximum value from this book.

Why This is About More Than *Just* Headlines

The Internet has shifted a lot of marketers and businesses to selling online. There are far fewer businesses that send out snail mail than there used to be. And since you might not be crafting a "sales letter" every day, you may not think you are constantly crafting headlines, but the truth is you are.

Now you may not refer to them as "headlines," but every blog post, email, newsletter, online article, and almost everything you write and share has a headline.

Think about Facebook posts, Twitter posts, LinkedIn updates and other social media posts. These are all small versions of the sales letter and understanding the psychology behind the perfect headline and how to create it are vital to getting engagement.

So don't be fooled into thinking that by learning how to craft the perfect headline you are only developing a skill set in one area. You can, and will, do a myriad of things with this formula that I am about to share with you.

And when you learn how to craft the perfect headline, you'll understand how to write better copy, too, so you can get more sales.

The Headline's Real Job - The Workhorse

I want to quickly fill you in on the real job that your headline needs to accomplish. There's been a lot written and said about what the headline should accomplish, and there's a lot of confusion about this topic.

Let me set the record straight – your headline does not need to sell your product. Let me say that again, your headline does not need to sell your product.

In fact it often doesn't need to mention your product at all. If you try and place all the selling burden on your headline, you are committing copywriting suicide.

Now I'm not saying that it isn't used in that way, or shouldn't be used in that way. There are many times where you will use it in that way, but you need to know when, and you need to know how.

It's easy to understand that the more of your copy that you can get the reader to read, the more likely they are to buy your product or service. So with that in mind, your headline has only one job.

Your headline's job is to get the attention of your audience, and get them to read the next line.

The same can be said about each line of copy you write, the goal should be to continue to keep the readers interest and force them to keep reading.

This understanding alone will be a huge help in your mission to get more sales. This understanding coupled with what I'm about to share with you, will allow you to craft headlines that convert like crazy.

And when you have headlines that convert like crazy you get more email opens, more blog readers and subscribers, more clicks to your content, more people reading your sales pages, and most importantly, more sales.

Okay, I think you get the idea. Let's get to work in crafting these headlines.

As a huge 'thank you' for picking up this book we've put together a headline swipe file that will put all others to shame.

It's got over 100 headline templates that you can use to start crafting your perfect headline.

Just head over to TheClickAuthority.com/headline1

CHAPTER 2

MARKET DESIRE

Think with me for a second about the forces of nature. The wind that can softly blow through your hair on a relaxing walk along the beach, or the hurricane that can literally pick your house up and move it 3 miles down the road.

Think about the light summer rain that can cool you down in sweltering heat, or the torrential downpour that can cause 10 ft floods and utter devastation.

Think about the smooth flow of a calm river, or the thundering of a massive waterfall.

Now it's not up to you or me to decided how these forces act. In a very real sense they are uncontrollable.

But even though we can't control them, we can, however, harness their power.

Now stick with me because this has everything to do with the first phase of crafting your perfect headline. In the same way that we can't change the forces of nature, we can only harness it, we can't control the direction, or desire, of the markets. The goal in crafting the perfect headline is to harness the power that already exists. In other words, harness what we like to call the "market desire."

It's well to note at this point that the things you're learning inside this book are incredibly powerful. And the steps I'm going to lay out for you are what we use every single day in our business. *Don't* short change yourself by skipping steps.

So let's dig deeper into market desire. First you must realize that your copy does not create market desire, market desire exists and is already in full force. It's your job to harness it to promote your message.

Just like the forces of nature, they exist and the only thing we can do is harness them, in no way can we change them.

You'll find that many struggling businesses are trying to create market desire. This is a losing battle. Find the market desire, and then attach your product or service to it.

If you don't attach yourself to the market desire, then you'll get slaughtered. You can either ride the tide of market desire or get crushed by its waves as they pass you by.

Time and time again we have seen this trend of businesses trying to go against market desire because they "know better. "

We did this for years with the messaging in one of our financial businesses. Instead of speaking to the market desire, we thought we knew what the consumer wanted to hear and what problems we thought we knew they were facing.

We continued to get slaughtered until we finally woke up to the idea that we needed to jump on the wave of market desire.

It was only after we stopped trying to educate our way to sales that we found success. We found the market desire, and we exploited it.

Before you can have hundreds, thousands, or even millions of people buying your product, you must first must have hundreds, thousands and millions of people that share the market desire that is satisfied by your product or service.

Because market desires are shared by millions of people, they can take many years to develop. They are never created by advertisers. I can't stress this enough. A market desire is held by hundreds, thousands and sometimes millions of people both publicly and privately.

Herein lies the power of marketing and advertising. If you can simply exploit that market desire not only will you engage those that share the desire publicly, but also those that share that market desire privately.

Let me give you an example.

The general public loves music. So when Apple created the iPod, and people could easily take music with them on the go, it satisfied a big market desire. It made carrying music super simple. This is market desire that was shared by millions, and Apple satisfied it. They made millions, if not billions, of dollars.

Let me give you another example.

Ever heard of Pepsi A.M.?

In the 80's Pepsi assumed that since people drink coffee they must like caffeine in the morning, hence their new product Pepsi A.M.

What they didn't quite realize though is that the market desire wasn't to have a soda drink in the morning, and the product was a complete flop.

So you must understand the market desire. And after you understand the market desire, you have to harness it.

So the next question is this: what are these market desires, and what is the force that creates them?

The Forces Of Market desire

There are two forces that create market desire.

First is a *fixed* force and the other is an *evolving* force.

Fixed forces are things that never change. The desire to be healthy or good looking, for example, are fixed forces of market desire. These fixed forces never change, and are common among all.

Evolving forces are far more difficult to nail down. Think of them as trends or fads.

It takes some intuition and foresight to recognize an upcoming trend and to be able to jump on the wave of market desire that will surely follow. If you can be intuitive enough to find these waves, you can make boat loads of money.

Understanding the market desire that you can hook your product to should be a daily exercise. Keeping up with trends, watching upcoming fads closely and crafting a message that ties your product to one market desire.

Okay now it's time for you to get out a pen. Your first job in crafting your killer headline is to define some of the forces (fixed or evolving) that create the market desire in your market. We will use this in upcoming chapters to help you see how you can exploit these market desires to sell more of the products and services you offer.

Step 1: Flesh Out The Forces Of Market Desire

Fixed Forces	Evolving Forces

Remember fixed forces are considered "timeless." The desire for women to be beautiful and thin. The desire for men to be masculine and tough.

Evolving forces are seen more as trends or fads. For example, the sudden desire to show your status with a brand new $50,000 boat instead of a swimming pool in the backyard, or the need to get out of the stock market because of an upcoming crash.

Take your time here and really flesh this stuff out. As you start to see and recognize the market desire, coming up with the direction for your sales pages and headlines is easier, and speaks more correctly to your audience.

Step 2: Start To Define Your Market Desire

The next step, after you've written out some of the forces driving market desire is to come up with the actual market desire that you will tie your product to.

Let me explain –
Let's say your product helps people get out of debt. Initially you might think the desire is to be debt-free but you have to think deeper.

Why would someone want to be debt-free?

Is it so they can feel less stress?

Is it so they can spend less time working and more time with their family?

You have to ask yourself "what is the root market desire that would drive someone to desire to be debt-free?"

Now before you try and come up with that on the first try, I will tell you that this is a process.

Start with what comes naturally and then think deeper about the desire that fits your product.

Remember, you are trying to exploit the market desire. Being debt free is the end game, the solution. The desire is something deeper, the pain of your customers, or the deep want of your customers.

Go ahead and give it a go. Remember you're after the most powerful market desire that can be tied to your product. I've found the best thing to do is write down the top 3-4 that come to mind and then we'll go to work from there.

As you're crafting this market desire there are a few things you should be thinking about.

What is the breadth of this desire? In other words, how many people share that same desire? Is it a small handful, or is it a huge mass?

The other is how quickly this group needs to fulfill this market desire. Is Mother's Day tomorrow and your market doesn't have flowers?

Step 3: Choose 1 Market Desire

This next step you take in crafting your headline is easily the most important and by far the most vital.

You need to decide which market desire is the strongest and most urgent for your customers right now.

Now look, undoubtedly your product will solve more than one

of the market desires you've come up with but you will do yourself a disservice if you try to cater to all of them in your headline. The key is to find the market desire that is the strongest, and use that in your headline, while splashing in the other desires throughout the rest of your copy.

This is where it pays to be "in the trenches. " If you are one of, or closely connected with, the individuals experiencing the market desire you are targeting, then it is easier to craft and focus this market desire.

If you aren't directly connected, then take the time to get as connected as possible. Study the target market, understand what they are thinking, try to live the market desire that they are experiencing.

Now that you've decided which market desire is strongest, let's jump into how to connect that market desire with your product or service in the most powerful way.

CHAPTER 3

FEATURES VS. BENFITS

Okay, now that you understand the market desire, your next task when crafting the headline is to drive home the market desire.

Don't leave anything to chance or speculation, be sure the market desire punches your reader in the face. Consider what, if anything, your reader knows about your product.

If your product is widely popular and well-known, then you can include it's name in your headline and follow-up with the market desire that it fulfills. If your product is unknown, focus on the market desire.

Regardless of whether or not your headline includes your product, it is incredibly vital that it intensifies the market desire that you have selected to target.

Here is your next pen and paper moment. You're going to analyze and break down your product and pull out every single benefit and feature you can come up with.

Understand that the difference between features and benefits is vital here.

Features are things like patent leather seating, a wide wheelbase, extra sensitive shocks. The benefit is a softer, smoother ride. Benefits speak much more loudly to the market desire then do the features of any product.

Your task is to start pulling out the features of your product and then we'll move on to identifying what benefit each of those features provide.

Features:

1.

2.

3.

4.

5.

6.

7.

When nailing down the features of your product think about what your product *is* versus what your product *does*.

It's the nails, the wood, the cement that make up a house. It's the machinery, the assembly line, etc.

Come up with as many features as you possibly can. The ones you think would be of most benefit to your market.

Once you've locked down those features, we now want to determine the benefit that each individual feature produces.

Let's talk about benefits. This is where the rubber really meets the road. At the end of the day people are not buying the wood, cement, and nails. They are buying a safe home, in a nice neighborhood, that provides them a safe, comfortable place to live.

In reality what your product *is* should never be the focus. Rather, what your product *does* should be the entire focus, then the features can be used support it.

So let's get crackin' – your next task is to turn each of those features into benefits. Go from what the product is to what it does.

I'll get your mind flowing with a quick sample using a computer as the product:

Feature	Benefit
Intel Core Duo Processor	Does what you need it to faster
Solid Titanium Body	Durable, long lasting
Retina Display	Clearer picture
100GB RAM	More storage, faster computer

Now it's your turn! Take the features you've already outlined and turn them into benefits:

Features Into Benefits

Feature 1:
  Corresponding Benefit:

Feature 2:
  Corresponding Benefit:

Feature 3:
  Corresponding Benefit:

Feature 4:
  Corresponding Benefit:

Feature 5:
  Corresponding Benefit:

Feature 6:
  Corresponding Benefit:

Feature 7:
  Corresponding Benefit:

Alright! Nice work! Now I want to help you take each of these benefits to the next level.

Your task at this point is to help the reader of your headline see, hear, taste, feel and smell what you're writing.

Start thinking about how you can intensify the benefits of your product. Let me give you a feel for what I mean while sticking with the computer example.

Benefit: Durable, long lasting
- This computer will outlast everything you can throw at it, it may even outlast you!
- The titanium body is smooth as silk but can withstand everything you throw at it.

Benefit: Retina Display
- A picture so clear you can see the pores on her face

Benefit: 100GB Ram
- Literally have you life flash before your eyes – you can store a life's worth of pictures on this hard drive
- A computer so fast, it will be waiting on you.

The examples could go on and on here and these are phrases that will come with time. As you get into the groove, so to speak, of crafting your headlines you'll be able to get more and more creative and really connect with you audience's senses.

It's these benefits that are unique to your product that will help you stand out among the crowd. This is especially true for those entering a crowded marketplace. Maybe your product does what others do, but much faster. Maybe your product is made from the purest of ingredients which, in turn, means longer-lasting, which will have your customer saying "I won't have to buy as much."

Again, the things your product *does* that are far more valuable than what your product *is*.

As you go about listing the features and connected benefits of your product, look for the benefit or the thing that your product does for its user that is most closely connected to the market desire you have chosen.

Even though there may be multiple benefits to choose from, your objective is to pick the one that best matches the market desire.

Let's do a quick recap of what we've covered so far:

- Good copywriting is incredibly powerful – it had me contemplating drop-kicking my iPhone off a cliff just to have a reason to get my hands on Amazon's new phone

- Learning how to craft headlines is about more than just headlines. You're learning how to speak to your audience and satisfy their desire.

- The headline's one job is to get readers to continue reading. Whether that means they open your email because of the subject, click on your blog post because of the title, or watch your video because of the title.

- Determining the strongest market desire to target is 100% crucial in crafting the perfect headline.

- We broke your product up into features and benefits.

- Benefits do the selling, features support it.

Alright! Onward we go!

Now that we've already determined the market desire that creates our marketplace our next 2 steps are to:

1. Determine our audience's understanding and awareness about your product and

2. Determine how often they are hit with a similar product offer.

CHAPTER 4

AWARENESS & REPETITION

Understanding how aware your audience is plays a big part in how you craft any headline.

If you're a huge, well known brand, your market is not being introduced to your product. In fact, your product may need no description at all.

This makes your headline easy to craft. All you may have to do in a headline is mention your product, offer a deep discount or special and you'll have crafted a headline that does it's job.

If you're not a huge, well known brand you'll obviously need to get more creative.

Let's take a look at the stages of awareness.

Very Aware.

If your audience is very aware of your product, they know what it is and are fairly certain they want it.

In this case your headline has a fairly simple job - mention your product and give huge incentive to buy it. ie. discount, sale, coupon, etc. As I mentioned, unless you're a huge brand you most likely won't find your audience in this state.

This state of awareness is uncommon, and is not likely where you'll be focusing.

Fairly aware.

In this case your audience is somewhat (not completely) aware of your product but still may be unconvinced it satisfies their desire.

In other words they know *of* the product but don't know quite yet that they want it. In this phase of awareness your are faced with the task of helping your prospect see the value in your product from a new or enhanced angle.

The simple suggestion that your product satisfies the market desire is no longer a viable strategy.

To enhance the image of your product you could do a few things:

1. Give an example of how your product has *already* solved the market desire.
    Example: "This Ugly Woman Had Beautiful Skin in Less Than 14 Days with ClearSkin"

2. Add proof.
    Example: "9 out of 10 stars use Dove Body Care for flawless looking skin."

3. Emphasize a recent enhancement to your product or service.

Example: "Announcing... The New Edition of the Encyclopedia that Makes it Fun to Learn Things."

4. Separate yourself from the competition.

Example: "When Your Financial Advisor Needs Advice, They Ask The Professionals at Vanguard."

5. Focus on a different benefit.

Example: "The New, Faster Smart TV means Less Searching and More Watching"

Unaware.

Many of you will find your audience is this state - and getting them from this state of unawareness to becoming customers is where the magic happens when it comes to crafting your headline.

In this state, your audience has no idea about you or your product. Therefore using your product name in the headline is likely not very effective.

While your prospect is unaware of your product, they are fully aware of the market desire your product solves.

So when crafting a headline for an unaware market, you *must* turn your focus to the market desire, and away from your product.

This is the most complex of all the states, and requires a thorough understanding of the market desire, and being able to clearly state it, along with the allure of a solution to that desire.

For most this art form is best seen in real life examples. Here copywriters have taken a shapeless desire and shaped it perfectly into a headline:

"Great New Discovery Kills Kitchen Odors Quick! Makes Indoor Air "Country-Fresh"

This headline speaks directly to the market desire, to kill kitchen odors. Notice it does a great job of adding the appeal of a "new discovery" to help the prospect see that they have not yet heard of it.

"How to Win Friends and Influence People"

This classic example speaks directly to the market desire. It's simple, and very powerful.

"Who Ever Heard of a Woman Losing Weight AND Enjoying 3 Delicious Meals at the Same Time?"

Again, a direct shot at the market desire. This headline strikes a chord with woman who want to lose weight but don't want to starve themselves, or radically change their diet to get there.

"Former Barber Earns $8,000 in Four Months As a Real Estate Specialist"

This example emphasizes how simple it is to be a real estate specialist by showing how a "barber" was able to earn $8,000 in 4 months.

"When Doctors 'Feel Rotten' This is What They Do"

This example uses an authority figure to help you visualize how incredibly powerful this solution is to feeling rotten. I mean, if a Doctor, who knows all about health and sickness, does it, why wouldn't I?

These are just a few examples of hundreds of successful headlines.

Download 100 of the top headlines of all time here:

http://theclickauthority.com/headline3

Now let's talk for a second about price. With an unaware market, the price of your product won't help you. The reader has nothing to compare it to.

In general people know what suit costs, so offering a suit for 5 bucks is obviously a sweet deal. Your unknown product, however has no track record, not buyer history, so claiming it's a 'killer deal' won't do much for you.

Once you've committed to writing this type of headline – one for the completely unaware crowd - your product, it's features, it's benefits simply fade into the background.

Your sole focus should be on the state of mind of your audience at this very moment. You are targeting an emotion and exploiting the heck out of it.

This is the headline, even more than the others, whose job it is to get the reader to read the second line.

Work to connect with your reader on a deep level with this type of headline - make it *his* problem, *his* state of mind.

Repetition

Next let's talk a little bit about repetition.

What you'll want to consider is how many times your target market has been hit with a similar product. If you are in the diet pill business, for example, you can be sure that your demographic has been hit with everything under the sun.

You're approach to this market will need to be one of pinpointing the most power benefit of your product, and driving it home with language your reader can taste, hear and feel. You have to do everything you can to separate your product from the product your market already knows about.

For the most part these products are related to a fixed force of market desire – the desire to reduce cholesterol for example.

There will always be a huge market of people looking to reduce their cholesterol. Some have tried multiple products and are fed up with poor results. Some are just looking for a solution but know there are thousands of options.

Either way they've all been hit with ad after ad and pitch after pitch of how to effectively reduce cholesterol and are growing numb to the constant promises and disappointment. You must take this into account when crafting the headline. More of the same will only hurt you.

To this point they have heard the outrageous claims made by competitors, they have stopped paying attention to the extreme examples and are looking for a new instrument with which to accomplish the goal.

This is where the 5 senses need to be present in your headline. A fresh approach to solving the problem is often the one that helps a customer visualize what your product will do for them.

Maybe your product has not already been beaten to death by everyone else and your market hasn't seen as many claims and gimmicks surrounding it.

In this case you want to take what's out there and working and make it better, make it your own. Yes I can reduce your cholesterol but it's more than that, I can do it in 21 days!

The awareness and state of repetition of your audience is constantly a work in progress. Keep this book handy as a reference as you continually analyze your audience's state of awareness and their state of repetition.

CHAPTER 5

WRITE, WRITE, WRITE

Congratulations for making it this far. Honestly it shouldn't have been that hard, this isn't a huge book. But I can promise you that by making it through this book you are ahead of 95% of your competition when it comes to copywriting.

Fact of the matter is there are very few people that take the time to do what you just did, and you'll see benefits *because* you took the time.

I wanted to quickly recap the main points in this book and then direct you to a couple awesome bonuses that I've put together exclusively for the readers of this book.

So here we go, let's look at some main takeaways from this book:

- Good copywriting is incredibly powerful – it had me contemplating drop-kicking my iPhone off a cliff just to have a reason to get my hands on Amazon's new phone. It's purpose it to get your prospects to understand what you offer, and make a decision.

29

- Learning how to craft headlines is about more than just headlines. You're understand what your prospect wants, and exploited that desire.

- The headline's one job is to get readers to continue reading. Whether that means they open your email because of the subject, click on your blog post because of the title or read your letter because of the title.

- Determining the strongest market desire to target is 100% crucial in crafting the perfect headline.

- We broke your product up into feature and benefits. Helping you realize it's the benefits that sell.

- We broke down the phases of awareness that you may find your audience in. How aware they are of your product make a big difference in how you craft a headline.

- Finally, we helped you determine how the phase of repetition your audience is in helps define the type of headline you create.

Writing killer copy is an art form and a skill that, like any other, takes perfecting. The key is practice and testing.

Let the numbers tell you how well you've done with your headline. If your email newsletter gets a 40% open rate after really thinking out the subject line, then work to replicate it's success the next time.

Good headlines are a key to success and powerful for your business – now get out there and start using them to grow your business!

As promised I wanted to provide you with some awesome extras simply because you picked up this book and gave it a shot.

The first is one that was mentioned earlier. It's the headline swipe file that puts all others to shame. This swipe file contains over 100 headline templates that can be used in any industry. All you have to do is plugin your product, it's benefits and see which one you like the best. Here's a few a my favorites:

Why I [blank] (And Maybe You Should Too)

What Everybody Ought to Know About [blank]

What Your [blank] Won't Tell You And How It Can Save You [blank]

Get over 100 headline ideas and templates by downloading the swipe file here: theclickauthority.com/headline1

Next I've got a list of 38 headline performance enhancers. These are some awesome ideas that give your headline that necessary shot in the leg. These are bound to increase the effectiveness of your headline – a few of my favorites:

Tie authority into the claim:
   The only golf ball used by Jack Nicklaus.

Stress the exclusivity of the claim:
   Only Crest has Scope – the only way to fresh breath all day long.

Warn the reader about possible pitfalls if he doesn't use the product:
   Don't hire a financial planner until you read this report.

Grab 35 more headline performance enhancers right here: theclickauthority.com/headline2

Finally I want to hook you up with a list of 100 of the greatest headlines ever written. This is perfect for headline inspiration and is an incredibly handy tool for putting headlines together.

Grab 100 of the greatest headlines ever written right here: theclickauthority.com/headline3

Contact information:

Nick Drzayich & Jake Thompson
TheClickAuthority.com
800-321-1636

www.ingramcontent.com/pod-product-compliance
Lightning Source LLC
Chambersburg PA
CBHW051225170526
45166CB00005B/2049